Lorikeet's in Love
Second Edition

Rainbow Lorikeets are so full of life, their fun-loving, mischievous nature is captivating.

This story, the ninth in the Lorikeet's Book Series for young readers, is based on a Lorikeet who meets his forever mate and falls in love.

Through my words and the creative vision of Lillian Falzon, whose illustrations brought these characters to life, I hope you enjoy a peek into the adventures of this quirky, colourful family.

It's Spring, the new leaves are opening on the trees and the gentle breeze gathers the old leaves and sweeps them softly to the ground.

Blossoms have burst from the buds in the trees and the bees are busily buzzing from blossom to blossom gathering nectar for honey.

An abundance of wildlife is in the garden, on the ground lizards are playing hide and seek amongst the rocks. Occasionally they freeze like statues with their heads held high, stretching and warming their bodies in the sun.

Larry (Lawrence Junior) is now a fully grown Rainbow Lorikeet and confidently flies off seeking adventure and no longer asks his brothers or sisters to join him.

Today, looking very handsome, Larry preens his green cloak and yellow and red vest. He shakes his head, fluffing up his blue cap and light green collar then stretches out his wings before he quietly leaves the nest.

Very soon after, Larry's parents, Lawrence and Loretta and Larry's siblings fly into the garden where the resident human has again replenished the sunflower seeds.

Larry is already in the garden and so is King Royce, Rosanna the Queen of Lorikeets and their family.

As usual everyone is enjoying eating the delicious seeds and flying around screeching and chattering, moving from tray to tray.

Larry looks up and notices Princess Rose.

Seeing Princess Rose gives Larry, a tingling feeling. He feels really strange and shakes his body, fluffing up his feathers.

He has seen Princess Rose many times, but for some reason today she looks very attractive dressed in her dusty pink robe, dazzling leafy tiara and jewelled collar.

Is he attracted to one of King Royce's daughters, Princess Rose?

Larry feels Princess Rose is the most beautiful Lorikeet in the garden, her brilliant red beak and her black eyes, so soft and inviting.

Larry not understanding these feelings, flies to his mother Loretta and explains his symptoms.

Larry says he is sick and is not sure what to do.

Loretta explains that the feeling he is having is normal and he isn't sick.

In Spring, male Lorikeets take notice and befriend female Lorikeets they like, that is how I met your father, Lawrence.

Larry still not sure about these strange feelings, flies over to where Princess Rose is eating. Her father, King Royce, is also on the tray.

Larry asks King Royce if it is ok for him to eat from the tray with them.

King Royce says "yes" and continues to eat the juicy seeds whilst keeping one eye on the mischievous Larry and his daughter, Princess Rose.

Larry's feelings are getting stronger the closer he is to Princess Rose. What has come over him?

He begins to sway, he bends his legs, puffs out his chest, bobs his head up and down and moves from side to side.

Being close to Princess Rose makes him feel warm and fuzzy and feel like dancing.

Princess Rose is a little surprised by this unexpected behaviour from Larry and flies into the tree nearby.

Larry follows Princess Rose to the nearby tree and continues dancing and bobbing on the branch next to her, gently caressing her wing.

After a while Princess Rose joins in and she and Larry are both bobbing up and down moving from side to side doing the special Lorikeet dance.

Lawrence and Loretta, Larry's parents, are watching on and realise that Larry is in love with Princess Rose.

Larry and Princess Rose spend the morning together sitting in a tree preening one another and chattering quietly.

Larry knows he has found a forever friend he wants to share the rest of his life with and seeks approval from King Royce.

King Royce and Rosanna, Queen of Lorikeets, accept
the union.

Lawrence and Loretta, fly over and join King Royce and
Rosanna, Queen of Lorikeets, on their tray.

Lawrence and Loretta are happy Larry their youngest
son has found a lifelong friend and support King
Royce's decision.

Princess Rose and Larry are recognised with a special ceremony.

All the Lorikeet families who visit the garden join in to congratulate them.

Larry and Princess Rose promise to stay together forever and continue to visit the garden as often as possible.

Lorikeet's in Love

ISBN

978-1-7642196-7-9 (Paperback)

978-1-7642196-8-6 (eBook)